What Is HTML CODE?

Spotlight on Kids Can Code

Patricia Harris

PowerKiDS press
New York

Published in 2018 by The Rosen Publishing Group, Inc.
29 East 21st Street, New York, NY 10010

Copyright © 2018 by The Rosen Publishing Group, Inc.

All rights reserved. No part of this book may be reproduced in any form without permission in writing from the publisher, except by a reviewer.

First Edition

Editor: Elizabeth Krajnik
Book Design: Michael J. Flynn

Photo Credits: Cover JGI/Tom Grill/Blend Images/Getty Images; p. 5 Rawpixel.com/Shutterstock.com; p. 6 https://commons.wikimedia.org/wiki/File:Dave_Raggett_cropped.jpg; p. 7 https://commons. wikimedia.org/wiki/File:Sir_Tim_Berners-Lee.jpg; p. 9 Africa Studio/Shutterstock.com; p. 11 Alena Ozerova /Shutterstock.com; p. 18 michaeljung/Shutterstock.com; p. 19 (wolf) miroslav chytil/Shutterstock. com; p. 21 24Novembers/Shutterstock.com.

Cataloging-in-Publication Data

Names: Harris, Patricia.
Title: What is HTML code? / Patricia Harris.
Description: New York : PowerKids Press, 2018. | Series: Spotlight on kids can code | Includes index.
Identifiers: ISBN 9781508155225 (pbk.) | ISBN 9781508155102 (library bound) | ISBN 9781508154273 (6 pack)
Subjects: LCSH: HTML (Document markup language)–Juvenile literature. | Internet programming–Juvenile literature. | Web sites–Juvenile literature.
Classification: LCC QA76.76.H94 H37 2018 | DDC 006.74–dc23

Manufactured in the United States of America

CPSIA Compliance Information: Batch #BS17PK: For Further Information contact Rosen Publishing, New York, New York at 1-800-237-9932

Contents

HTML Basics 4

The History of HTML 6

Text Editors for Writing HTML 8

Sample Program 10

Making Modifications to HTML 14

Adding Photos to Web Pages 16

Make Your Own Web Page 18

Don't Forget! 20

Glossary 23

Index 24

Websites 24

HTML Basics

HTML is one of the most important coding systems in the world. Behind every web page is a page of HTML code. HTML, or hypertext markup language, is a markup language used to create web pages. Markup languages are computer languages that are made for working with text. Markup languages provide a **format** for text files. This determines the text's style and the layout of the web page.

The codes for formatting are called tags. They're called tags because they use special characters—also called tags—to hold the formatting commands. In HTML, the tag characters are < to start the formatting code and > to end it. An example of tags in HTML is <html> to tell where the HTML file starts and </html> to tell where the file ends. The chart on page 5 shows some of the more common HTML tags.

Web pages play an important role in our everyday lives. Without HTML code, businesses wouldn't be able to create or maintain their websites.

`<h1>…</h1>`	top-level heading
`<b>…</b>`	**bold**
`<u>…</u>`	<u>underline</u>
`<i>…</i>`	*italics*
`<p align=left>…`	left-aligned text
`<p>…</p>`	new paragraph
`<hr>`	horizontal line
` `	line break

The History of HTML

In 1980, computer scientist Tim Berners-Lee became interested in creating a system researchers could use to share information. This idea led to something even larger—the World Wide Web. HTML is the publishing language for the World Wide Web, which means it's used to create the web pages we see. Berners-Lee also created HTML.

HTML needs to work on all the different types of computers that are connected to the Internet. It also needs to work with the different publishing methods on each of these computers. HTTP, or hypertext transfer **protocol**, is

In 1992, Dave Raggett, a researcher for Hewlett-Packard, visited Berners-Lee to further **develop** HTML. After he returned to England, Raggett created a better **version** of HTML called HTML+. HTML has been improved several times. At present, HTML5 is the version most commonly used.

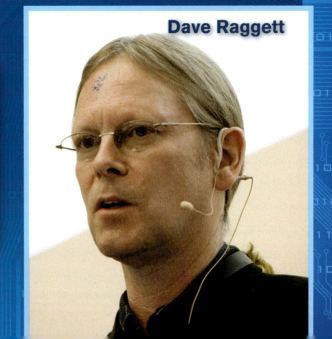

Dave Raggett

Breaking the Code

Most people think that the Internet and the World Wide Web are the same thing, but they aren't. The Internet is a network that connects millions of computers all over the world. The World Wide Web is a way people share information over the Internet. Without the Internet, the World Wide Web would not be possible.

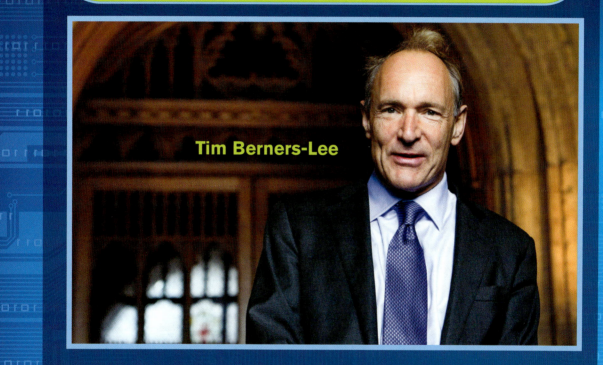

Tim Berners-Lee

the way files are retrieved, or brought back, from an Internet-connected computer.

Berners-Lee encouraged other people to work to make the World Wide Web and HTML better. In September 1991, he created the WWW-talk mailing list, which allowed people to share their ideas.

Text Editors for Writing HTML

You can write your HTML code in a text editor and have it run in your **browser**. That's the way early web page coders worked. On a Windows-based computer, you can use Notepad and, on a Mac, you can use Syntra Small. You just type in your code and save it with a file name that ends with .htm or .html. Remember where you store the file.

Another way to write your code is to work in a special **environment** for writing and running code. CodeMirror is a text editor that tells you if there are missing coding elements. CodeRun is an integrated development environment (IDE) that allows you to work within your browser whether you're on a computer or a tablet. Codeanywhere is an IDE that helps you write your code and gives you information about your code as you write it.

Software is a set of instructions or a program that instructs a computer what to do. CodeMirror is open-source software for coding in your browser. Open-source software is software you can use for free. It can be used to code with HTML and other programming languages.

9

Sample Program

A good way to start learning about coding in HTML is to study a sample program. Here's a simple program for printing out the words "Hello world!" In the example on the next page, you can see how tags are used in HTML. You will see that tags are nested under, or used within, other tags.

The first step when coding with HTML is to type <!DOCTYPE html>. This states what type of **document** you're creating. Although it looks like an HTML tag, it just tells the browser that you are writing a file in HTML5. This opening line is followed by: <html> (the opening tag), which says the file is now starting. At the end, you see </html> (the closing tag), which says this is the end of the file. Almost all opening tags in HTML require a closing tag.

```
1    <!DOCTYPE html>
2    <html>
3    <head>
4        <title>This is a title</title>
5    </head>
6    <body>
7        <p>Hello world!</p>
7    </body>
8    </html>
9
```

The output of your HTML code appears on your browser screen. Output is the information produced by a computer.

Between the tags <head> and </head> and <body> and </body>, the information is **indented** so it's easier to see the nested tags. The opening tag <head> tells the browser that what follows is not to be shown on the screen. It is followed by the tag <title> to say this is the title that appears in the browser tab for this page but not on the actual page.

The line that has <p>Hello world!</p> tells the browser screen to show the sentence "Hello world!" The tags <p> and </p> indicate that these words make a paragraph.

In simple HTML documents, you can use special tags to describe how the text and background should look. If the line <p>Hello world!</p> was rewritten as <p>Hello<strong>world</strong>!</p>, "world" would appear in bold print. The tag <strong> is an HTML5 tag that is preferred to the old <b>, or bold, tag.

This is heading 1
This is heading 2
This is heading 3
This is heading 4
This is heading 5
This is heading 6

```
1
2
3  <h1>This is heading 1</h1>
4  <h2>This is heading 2</h2>
5  <h3>This is heading 3</h3>
6  <h4>This is heading 4</h4>
7  <h5>This is heading 5</h5>
8  <h6>This is heading 6</h6>
```

HTML has six levels of headings that can be used for your output. The tag <h1> is used for the top level. You can use headings to show lines of text in different sizes. They should only be used for separate headings, not for text in paragraphs.

Making Modifications to HTML

In the past, HTML included tags to change **fonts** or colors for web page text or backgrounds. This wasn't too difficult for simple web pages. However, it was more difficult to use these for **complex** web pages. A new system called Cascading Style Sheets (CSS) was added to HTML5. CSS states how elements will appear on a screen and can be applied to several screens. Web designers can even store style sheets—or style guidelines for commonly used fonts and layouts—in separate files and use them for many web pages.

If you want to add your CSS rules right into your HTML file, you add code to the <head> part of your file. You would add the tag <style>. This code would be followed by any style rules you want to use. It would end with </style>. The style tag can also be used to insert a rule right in the line of HTML code, but then the rule only works for the code between the tags.

14

```
 1    <head>
 2        <style>
 3        body {
 4          background-color: lightblue;
 5          }
 6
 7        h1 {
 8            color: white;
 9            text-align: center;
10        }
11
12        p {
13            font-family: verdana;
14            font size: 20px;
15        }
16        </style>
17    </head>
```

This CSS code has been written in an HTML editor that shows the various parts of the code in color. This code would apply to all top-level headings and paragraphs included in your code.

Adding Photos to Web Pages

Web pages look better when you include pictures. HTML allows you to do that. The pictures must be stored in the same place your HTML file is located. Make sure your image works well with your text and don't forget to check about photo **copyright**.

You use the <img> tag to include pictures on your website. The line might look like this:

```
<img src ="house.gif" alt="house picture" height="42"
width="42">
```

"Src"—which is short for "source"—lets you name the file for the picture. "Alt" lets you add text that tells what the picture is in case the picture doesn't load correctly. The height and width set the size of the picture.

To create a link to an image on another web page, you use the form:

```
<a href="http://www.webpage.com">words for the link name
that shows on the web page</a>
```

It's important to make sure your text and pictures support each other. If they don't, your **audience** may get confused.

Make Your Own Web Page

Now it's your turn to create a simple web page using HTML. First you must plan what you want to code. You can create a simple web page with your name in color, a sentence you feel is important, a link to an existing web page that you like, and a picture from your own files.

The web page you create will be on your own computer, not on the Internet, so no one will be able to see it except for you. The environment you'll use is just the text editor on your computer. (See page 8.) You'll create a folder on your desktop to hold your HTML file and your picture file. Remember to start your HTML file with the required opening. (See page 10.)

I am called Wolf Coder

My favorite saying is:

To live wild and free also means having a pack.

A web page about wolves

This web page includes a heading in color, an important sentence, a link to a web page, and a picture. Need more help coding your own page? Go to page 22 to see the code for this page.

Don't Forget!

After you've thought about the content of your web page, you'll also need to think about the style you want for your page. You'll want to think about things like background color, text size, and text color. While you're coding your web page, you'll want to look at the results as you go to be sure your code reflects your plan.

One thing some HTML coders sometimes forget is the saying, "Just because you can doesn't mean you should." You can add many font changes and font colors to your web page, but too many fonts and too many colors can **distract** from your content. The text, pictures, and links on your page are important. Don't let a busy **presentation** take away from your content.

20

LETters **in** different **FONTS** **and** colors ARE distracting!

If fonts and colors distract your audience, they may not actually read your content. They may even leave your web page and find another one that is easier to read.

Code for Web Page from Page 19

```html
1    <!DOCTYPE html>
2    <html>
3    <head>
4        <title>My first coded web page</title>
5        <style>
6            h1 {color:blue;}
7        </style>
8    <head>
9    <body>
10       <h1>I am called Wolf Coder</h1>
11       <img src="wolf.jpg" alt="wolf picture"
             style=height="150" width="150">
12       <p>
13       <p>My favorite saying is:
14       </p>
15       <p>To live wild and free also means having a
          pack.</p>
16       <p>
17       <p>
18       <a href="https://en.wikipedia.org/wiki/Gray_wolf">A
          web page about wolves</a>t
19       </p>
20   </body>
21   </html>
```

Glossary

audience: Those people who give attention to something said, done, or written.

browser: A computer program that allows users to search the Internet.

complex: Having many parts.

copyright: The legal right to be the only one to reproduce, publish, and sell the contents and form of a literary or artistic work.

develop: The act of building, changing, or creating over time.

distract: To draw a person's thoughts or attention to something else.

document: A computer file containing data entered by a user.

environment: The combination of computer hardware and software that allows a user to perform various tasks.

font: A set of characters of the same design that are a certain size and style.

format: A general plan for how something should be organized or arranged.

indent: To set in from the margin, or the part of a page or sheet outside the main body of print or writing.

presentation: The way in which something is arranged, designed, or presented.

protocol: A set of rules or processes for sharing data between computers.

version: A form of something that is different from the ones that came before it.

Index

B
Berners-Lee, Tim, 6, 7
browser, web, 8, 9, 10, 11, 12

C
Cascading Style Sheets (CSS), 14, 15
Codeanywhere, 8
CodeMirror, 8, 9
CodeRun, 8
copyright, 16

E
environment, 8, 18

F
font, 14, 20, 21

H
headings, 5, 13, 15, 19
Hewlett-Packard, 6
HTML+, 6
HTML5, 6, 10, 12, 14
HTTP, 6

I
integrated development environment (IDE), 8

M
Mac, 8
markup languages, 4

N
Notepad, 8

O
output, 11, 13

R
Raggett, Dave, 6

S
software, 9
Syntra Small, 8

T
tags, 4, 10, 12, 14
text editor, 8, 18

W
Windows, 8
World Wide Web, 6, 7

Websites

Due to the changing nature of Internet links, PowerKids Press has developed an online list of websites related to the subject of this book. This site is updated regularly. Please use this link to access the list: www.powerkidslinks.com/skcc/html